APPOMATTOX
and Other Poems

APPOMATTOX
and Other Poems

Robert Amsey Merritt

EXPOSITION PRESS   HICKSVILLE, NEW YORK

FIRST EDITION

© 1979 by Robert Amsey Merritt

All rights reserved, including the right of reproduction in whole or in part, in any form or by any means, electronic or mechanical, including photocopying, recording, or by any information storage and retrieval system. No part of this book may be reproduced without permission in writing from the publisher. Inquiries should be addressed to Exposition Press, Inc., 900 South Oyster Bay Road, Hicksville, N.Y. 11801.

ISBN 0-682-49184-5

Printed in the United States of America

To the reader, my wife, Louise, and my family, my relatives by blood and marriage, and my friends and acquaintances—in the optimistic hope that this book may be entertaining, informative, and stimulating to you, and that it may help each of you to better comprehend and appreciate all that we have inherited.

May it also encourage all of you, as citizens, to always work for good, efficient, representative government at the local, state, national, and, finally, world levels through the United Nations, where all peoples of the earth have a common vital interest, and, I contend, all are, or should be, citizens, by virtue of the membership of their respective nations.

I acknowledge with grateful appreciation the kind and efficient assistance, help, and encouragement given me by Mr. Edward Uhlan, Publisher; Mr. Ronald Guzik, Advertising Director; Mr. Alonzo H. Smith, Vice President, Sales and Promotion; Ms. Joanne Reilly, Sales and Promotion; Ms. Muriel Vitriol, Managing Editor; and Ms. Annette Corkey, my individual Editor, in compiling this material and producing this book.

Contents

Introduction	9
Appomattox	11
Number Thirty-six	12
Sedgefield Fox Hunt	13
Robert Burns	14
A College Student's Song about Greensboro Colleges	15
The Mockingbird	16
March at Jefferson Square	17
Greensboro	18
Washington	20
Navy's Norfolk, Virginia, B.O.Q., S.P. 17	21
High Point—Greensboro Furniture Dealers' Song	22
The Reading Prodigy	23
Said	25
Tennessee Volunteers of 1951	26
Boston Common	27
On Law, the Universal Law	28
The Spread of Law	29
The Train Trip	31
Mortal You	34
Higher Law	35
Westward Friendly, Ho!	36
Spring from the Southeastern Building	37
The Eastern Regional Tournament	38
The Mount Airy Train	39
On the Way to the Moon	40
The Moon Landing	41
Those Interplanetary Men	41
The Descent to the Moon	42
The Candidate for the Senate	43
Easter	44
Unite	45
Our United Nations	46

Bob Fitzsimmons	47
The Constitution	51
Old Pomona Streetcar Line at Greensboro	57
Back in the Good Old Days	63
Halloween, on an Old Streetcar	64
Judge Lon McGraw	65
Snow Blizzard	68
Two-Way Elm	70
Early Spring	71
A Great World Christmas Tree	72
That Day	73
Spaceman John Glenn's Ride	75
Washington and Lee	77
Virginia	78
The 1952 Presidential Race and Former Races	79
Peter Francisco and Guilford Courthouse	82
The Valley Dale Wreck	87
The Criminal Term (Long Ago)	88
At Another Criminal Term (In the Distant Past)	90
At Still Another Criminal Term (Many Years Ago)	91
At the Criminal Term—The Last Case (An Ancient Term)	92
Index of Names and Titles	96

Introduction

These poems cover a very wide variety of subjects for discussion. Many are about Greensboro and the area surrounding it. Others deal with the state of North Carolina, the other states, our nation and other nations, and the world. Many focus on people, places, and events, while others are concerned with the development of laws, governments, nations, constitutions, and the world federation, or United Nations.

Some of these poems are concerned with the past, others with the present and the future. Some are narrative poems. Others are lyric and, I feel, suitable to be put to music; these were in fact written with a certain tune in mind, as indicated.

Many of the poems are fictional and may be partly or entirely imaginary or legendary, or any combination of these.

In those cases where known names, places, and facts are used, accuracy has been attempted; however, in a few instances, some poetic license has been utilized for the sake of emphasis.

Appomattox

Two stalwart men met there that day,
At the McLean House, on April 9, 1865;
Though one surrendered to the other,
After four years of war,
'Twas superbly done;

The loser was a winner at the table;
The victor met him as a brother,
Declined his sword, and disbursed food—
Let him and all his men go free,
Even let them keep their side arms and their horses,
Just took their word they would no longer fight the Union,
A promise which the losers have kept well for a hundred years
And their descendants should for many hundred more.

Two gallant men met there, that day,
At the McLean House: Grant and Lee—
Arranged the Peace that Lincoln sought,
And put a "Great Experiment" on its course again.

Number Thirty-six

It's past high noon on a clear September day,
And "uptown" Greensboro is two miles away.
A faint autumn breeze stirs our dusty lawn and seeks to pass;
Bob, a big yardman, mows our grass.
A ripsaw, working at capacity at a planing mill, far off,
Up along the railroad, sounds like a large dry fly—

In the distance, there's a faint whistle;
We barely hear it—then silence—
A little later, another whistle, a moan—much louder and longer—
Then silence again—
Next—a long mellow blow—
Moving closer and at great speed—
As Bob's mowing machine clatters across the lawn.
Now, there's another blow, loud, mellow, and long, and yet another,
And a ringing bell,
And soon the sound of rushing drivers' wheels and clanking cars;
The ground shakes beneath us.
"Thirty-six is a-rollin'," hollers Bob;

We run and look up Kenilworth Street to the railroad—
Now there's a long, loud whistle blast.
A large brassy steam engine flashes 'cross the street
Amid a cloud of steam and dust, two hundred yards away;
And then the coal car and zigzagging profiles of baggage
And express cars, day coaches (with squeals) and more day coaches,
Pullman cars, a dining car, and more Pullman cars,
And lastly, the golden Observation Platform for a flash—
And then it's gone—leaving a small trailing hurricane
Of dust and dirt and blowing bits of paper and debris;

Excited college girls, for the fall terms are on board,
Arriving rapidly on Thirty-six, the Pride of the Southern.

Sedgefield Fox Hunt*

Here at Sedgefield! Here at Sedgefield!
Shivering in the early morn,
As we line up for the Fox Hunt,
Summoned hither by the horn.

Now it blasts out—now we charge forth—
Horses gallop 'cross the fields,
'Cross the rolling hills of Guilford,
After dogs that are baying loud.

Soon a green stretch—then a small wood,
Where we dodge the limbs and brush,
By a wheat field—down a steep slope,
Fast we ride on in the rush.

O'er a rail fence—near a golf course,
Into Sedgefield's grazing grounds,
Jump the small stream—up the creek bank,
Follow frantic barking hounds.

Soon he flounders—now he's headed;
Now he's cornered near a hill.
Fast we gallop through the sagebrush,
Swing dismounted at the kill.

Here at Sedgefield! Here at Sedgefield!
While as yet 'tis early morn,
We've been summoned to the Fox Hunt;
We've responded to the horn.

---

*Sing to the tune of "Clementine."

Robert Burns*

There in Scotland—in the highlands,
Struggling on those rugged slopes,
With a bold song and a free note,
Lived the Scotch Poet, Robert Burns.

Rustic genius—hard he labored,
As he read from nature's hand,
Great his love songs—deep his insight,
Flowing from his native land.

While a plowman, on the hillsides,
Countless folk songs he unfurled,
His fair loves—like Queens of Scotland—
Took the stage and thrilled the world.

He was poet of the people,
A democracy his dream,
Cast a fond glance at the U.S.,
And to go there was his dream.

Thanks to him, first son of Scotland,
Higher yet our spirit turns;
With his folk songs—and his free note,
Bard of Scotland, Bobby Burns.

---
*Sing to the tune of "Clementine."

A College Student's Song
about Greensboro Colleges*

We'll wind up exams,
And soon, I'll go to Greensboro,
That great college town of fair women—
To see a charming College Girl,
The very prettiest in the world,
A brunette with brown eyes, from 'way down East.†

We'll enter the city
From a broad superhighway;
The flowers in the yards will be blooming—
And the tender green grass,
Over all out-of-doors,
Will be notice enough that it's Springtime.

The girls will be walking,
About the Main Buildings,
Displaying their newly bought finery—
Like an Easter Parade—
Such pulchritude galore,
What a time for tired eyes to get rested.

We'll stroll 'round the front lawn,
And drive out to Starmount,
And later return about sunset—
She'll be the Queen of Charm,
That night at the Spring Prom,
And 'twill be Royal Music, we dance to.

---

*Sing to the tune of "Loch Lomond."
†Repeat verse 1 for the final verse.

The Mockingbird

Singing away goes the mockingbird,
High on a limb in the apple tree,
Giving all the world a lift,
Setting all its creatures free.

A busy, twittering, mocking man,
Fast mocking everything he can,
Full and bursting o'er with song,
Look and hear the one-man band.

So light and feathery fly his notes,
A free performance for us all,
An extrovert and unashamed,
Welcome, friends, and heed his call.

His throne, the treetops high in the air,
His broadcasting station's 'way up there;
A ne'er-ending stream of Heavenly Notes,
The King of Song—we cast our votes.

Singing away goes the mockingbird,
High on a limb in the apple tree,
Giving all the world a lift,
Setting all its creatures free.

March at Jefferson Square*

Just walking down the sidewalk,
On the way to Jefferson Square,
The skirts are whipping skyward;
Don't you wish that you were here?

See college girls and town girls,
Pretty struggling everywhere,
As they fight those mid-March breezes,
That blow 'round Jefferson Square.

What curves! What consternation!
Bodies beautiful everywhere!
Frantic females fight the breezes,
In the battle at Jefferson Square.

What will the next wind bring us?
What will the next blast blow?
I can't find words to tell you,
You shouldn't miss the show.

Now wasn't it nice at any price,
As they helped their business grow,
To build a tall skyscraper,
That makes the breezes blow?

Mid-March at Greensboro,
On a walk near Jefferson Square,
The skirts are whipping skyward;
Don't you wish that you were here?

---

*Sing to the tune of "The Bonnie Banks of Clyde with My Lassie by My Side."

Greensboro*

Hail the Spirit of Seventy-six!
Forward march with Greensboro,
Center of the Old North State,
A citadel of Freedom!

Nathanael Greene outfought him here
At the Battle of Guilford Courthouse;
Lord Cornwallis lost a third,
Compelling "Quits" at Yorktown.

Our Town was born in Eighteen Eight,
Three Hundred people chartered,
Grown in Nineteen Seventy-six
To a Hundred and Fifty-five Thousand.

Ardent couples loving life,
Step up the population;
Within another hundred years,
We're apt to have a million.

Here's a Southern College Zone,
Strong for education,
Girls and boys from many Lands,
Cross section of creation.

Here's a thriving business life;
We trade and manufacture,
Insure, and have a thousand firms,
With specialties aplenty.

Landing in the varied lights,
Planes from all directions—
Huge Airport in the Piedmont Hills,
Key link for wide connections.

---

*Sing to the tune of "Yankee Doodle."

Quick to fight for human rights,
Vigilant and ready,
Sight of Pete Francisco's Stand,*
And home of George E. Preddy.†

Democratic to the core,
Athens of the Southland,
Here the blacks won civil rights,
At Woolworth's sit-down counters.

We're in the fight for Women's Rights,
For minorities and majorities,
Grant each cause its honest due,
With all of its just priorities.

Heaven help our Patriot City live,
True to Guilford Courthouse,
And win for Freedom's Holy Cause,
New victories for all people.

Hail the Spirit of Seventy-six!
Forward march with Greensboro,
Center of the Old North State,
A citadel of Freedom!

---

*Pete Francisco was a Virginia giant who killed eleven British soldiers at the Battle of Guilford Courthouse (Greensboro, N.C.), on March 15, 1781, during the Revolutionary War.

†Major George E. Preddy, Jr., was a U.S. Air Force fighter pilot in World War II, who brought down twenty-eight enemy planes in the air and destroyed five on the ground. The leading American Ace, he was tragically killed at the Battle of the Bulge, December 25, 1944, by our own anti-aircraft fire.

Washington

We're moving down a large stream,
That wide, enchanting river,
That flows and winds forever,
Past monuments and mansions,
And glides on by Mount Vernon.

We finally reach the large wharf,
And turn in for the mooring,
Then walk the graveled pathway,
That winds the bluff or hilltop,
Up to the stately mansion.

We try the long white front porch,
Two-story high veranda,
And look across the green lawn,
On to the wide Potomac,
That flows on by Mount Vernon.

Horn blasts upon the warm wind,
Boats passing on the river,
Blow greetings to Mount Vernon,
In honor of its owner,
The Father of our Nation.

And crowds of faithful people,
Walk each day through the mansion,
Through all surrounding buildings,
And lastly to the plain tomb,
That's labeled, "Washington."

He fought five years for freedom,
Helped form our Federal System,
With self-rule by our people,
A Bill of Rights for each man—
Broad pattern for each nation.

Free peoples of all nations,
While passing on life's river,
Blast greetings to Mount Vernon,
To glorify forever,
The life of Washington.

Navy's Norfolk, Virginia, B.O.Q., S.P. 17*

The Navy has a B.O.Q. in Norfolk.
Its spacious lawn in front is solid green;
Twelve high columns square away its veranda.
I like to stay at S.P. 17.

Through the Lobby, by the desk, into the Wardroom,
Where the Steward points the way to your seat,
As his mates are marching in from the Galley
With platters full of food for you to eat.

And let me say a word about their breakfasts;
Just check off any items on the cards:
Honeydew, hotcakes, ham and eggs, or bacon—
That food is fit to set before the gods.

My girl will ne'er forget their luscious dinners,
The sweetest steak her tooth did ever try,
With tender vegetables and Waldorf salad,
And crowned with melting cream on apple pie.

The Navy has a B.O.Q. in Norfolk.
Its spacious lawn in front is solid green;
Twelve high columns stand around its veranda.
I like to stay at S.P. 17.

---

*Sing to the tune of "Little Bright Eyes, Will You Miss Me?"

High Point—Greensboro Furniture Dealers' Song*

We've started from Greensboro,
All fast bound for High Point,
America's Furniture City,
With new furniture and furnishings,
Made to lift us all,
To new heights of beauty,
Ne'er dreamed of.

Now, our friends take the old road,
But we take the new road,
And we'll be in High Point afore them;
On this sunny day in May.
We'll glide the Super Way—
Rolling hills and dense woods,
Soon flit by us.

We arrive at the outlet,
And turn north on Main Street,
That wide business way through the city,
And stop at the massive building,
To see the great displays,
Find our friends of the trip
Haven't arrived yet.

But soon from the old road,
At last through the stoplights,
Our late friends blushingly enter,
Marveling at the Exhibition,
And greeting many buyers,
And we all tour the displays,
Together.

---

*Sing to the tune of "Loch Lomond."

In mid-Carolina,
'Mid flowers of Good Guilford,
Just fifteen miles from each other,
We're closely bound together,
No matter whatever,
Our great cities:
High Point and Greensboro.

The Reading Prodigy

'Twas Curry's third-grade class,
Every story a thriller,
Nobody could read
Like Mary Lou Miller.

Some stammered, some stuttered,
Some halted along,
But she read as smooth,
As a mockingbird's song.

A young beauty herself who made beauty with words,
She read Aesop's Fables,
"The Crow and the Pitcher,"
"The Fox and the Grapes."

Still on without hindrance,
She read as she stood,
Halfway through the adventures
Of Bold Robinhood.

I admired her fluency,
Completely, you bet,
And would gladly be listening,
If she were reading there yet.

Fascinating, each topic,
The suspense, the lure,
How pleasant if she'd take us,
Through all literature.

Of the third-grade readers,
None was ever finer,
In the entire expanses
Of Old North Carolina.

But suddenly she vanished,
Far down time's corridor,
When her folks moved away
To the Fair State of Florida.

'Twas quite overwhelming;
My spirits sank low.
She disappeared in the past,
Over forty years ago.

A dark, cruel day, I still recall it with pain,
But I've dipped in the past and reflected again—
"Our stroke of bad luck
Was the Flower State's gain."

I figure she's a good reason
Florida has boomed:
With Mary Lou reading to 'em,
Their knowledge has zoomed.

Said

Forsooth this story you must know,
Took place three hundred years ago,
A novice over-fond of "said,"
Played havoc with his learned head.

At first he used this odd device,
Just here and there—and found it nice,
To tie and hold a noun or two,
And show them legal through and through.

To draw a contract or a deed,
He pitched in "said," his friend in need;
To start along a hard divorce,
"Said" launched and kept it on its course.

"Said's" toehold on a noun or two,
Increased from that to two times two,
Again from that to four times four,
Geometric progress o'er and o'er.

At length "said" was a super word,
The greatest, grandest ever heard,
Then half the words he spoke were "said";
Two-thirds of those he wrote were "said."

Tight pressured in his skull was "said,"
An atom processed for the blast,
Long tick—then off it went at last—

An awful flash, a great light showed,
A mushroom coiled, and belched and glowed;
Ten miles through gusts he rose and whirled,
And straight into the "loonyworld."

A novice over-fond of "said,"
Played havoc with his learned head.

Tennessee Volunteers of 1951

You, Volunteers! You, Neylanders!
You've met both Wing and Tee;
Your cleats have flashed o'er turf and goal,
As you've run for Tennessee.

On Shields-Watkins Field, on rivals' grids,
You've charged each hostile clan;
Your Touchdown exploits rush the breeze,
To a football-hungry land.

Lauricella and Reichicar,
Fast backs with dash and brawn,
A snap back through the center's arch,
A bullet pass; one's gone.

Tackle Pearman and Guard Daffer,
And the whole battering line,
All snatching ends and speedy backs,
That make up the great machine.

Your current victories take the land,
Raise high your famous name,
Even higher than Michigan State,
Even higher than Notre Dame.

Ten times you've met a gallant foe;
Ten times immerged the winner,
And so atop the A.P. Poll,
There floats your great Volunteer Banner.

You, Volunteers! You, Neylanders!
Quite well you've fought your way,
Leathered Squadron from the Southern Hills,
Grid Champs of the U.S.A.

Boston Common*

Cuss the torrid heat of summer,
As we swelter, sweat, and simmer;
In the middle part of Boston—
What a green expanse to rest on;
Many a man and often a woman,
Fain has dropped on Boston Common.
Close by the walkway as we pass,
Hundreds near prostrate on the grass—
Acres of people, folk from around,
Have seized the shade spots and dropped to the ground;
With melting faces, hard-breathing noses,
They're stretching in quite varied poses,
Many horizontal on the Common,
In a free land, each his own plan.

---

*Impressions received while walking across the famous Boston Common one night while attending the American Bar Association Convention from August 23 to August 28, 1953, before air conditioning was very much in use, and while a spell of extremely hot weather had set in.

On Law, the Universal Law

World citizen, world friend—
What reaches into all parts of the world
And brings the blessings of life and liberty to all people?
What invention of man lifts the human race up by its bootstraps?
What great dome is big enough to hold all of our loftiest ideals,
And is the only means whereby man can possibly regulate himself and all nations?

Much of the best of our philosophy and religion has been wasted these many years,
And has had no universal application—
Before the United Nations.

The Spread of Law

At first there was no plan of Law,
And early man lived by tooth and claw,
In caveman style—a life in the raw,
In death-dealing jungle awe.

And then man took to family groups,
And family customs: rude family laws—
But except for the family, the World Jungle persisted.

And after thousands of years—
To Tribal Groups and crude Tribal Law,
But outside of the Tribe, the World Jungle persisted.

And after aeons of time,
To City Groups and City Laws—
But outside of the City, the World Jungle persisted.

And then after being further lost in time,
To Nations' Groups and Nations' Laws,
But outside of the Nations, the World Jungle persisted.

And finally some Nations grew large and devoured others,
And spread to the New World, and divided and grew—
And some Nations had one-man laws of the Dictator, or laws of an
   absolute oligarchy,
And others tended toward laws of the people,
And this is the Battle Point at which we now struggle—
But outside of the Nations, the World Jungle still persists—
Except that there has been started
An Association of Nations: a UNITED NATIONS,
Thanks to the Nations and Roosevelt, Churchill, Rockefeller,
   Wilson, and many others.

But this last large group is yet vaporous, largely formless,
And has not congealed—
True, it may have helped to calm down the Jungle of the World—

But it's now too weak, and built against itself too much to be a world
    policeman—
It's only a baby beachhead, planted on the shore of a flaming planet,
Holding nebulously as mammoth hostile forces group to crush it—
The atom bomb, the missile age, the interplanetary thrusts—
Have swept upon us with great suddenness.

Only a worldwide structure, with a worldwide constitution,
  With its Bill of Rights and responsibilities for individuals and
    nations,
And with democratic laws in it and the nations comprising it,
Founded on ethics, education, and a sense of the universal dignity of
    man,
And good democratic people throughout the entire world,
Can save us from World War III and genocide.
Without Law we have nothing,
All of civilization that is and will be must rest upon the Law.

We need a fairer and more enlightened World Constitution:
A sounder Law Home for all mankind—
A worldwide plan with checks and balances drafted for the people
    and by the people—
A United Nations strong and great,
The hope of man—with halls of state
Where world congresses or parliaments shall meet and legislate
    sovereign laws
On a worldwide basis, and provide for a world police force and for
    world protection,
Leaving all of the remaining powers to the Nations or the people,
And creating a government where many evils of petty nationalism
    shall wither into nothingness, and where many must be tolerated,
As this planetary life becomes stronger and greater,
And pushes on to other worlds.
Defend and improve the United Nations!

The Train Trip

All aboard! The whistle blows; the bell rings loud—
An instant stillness hits the crowd.
A sudden swish, the suspense grows;
A rumbling noise, Vesuvius blows.
The big wheels turn; each rail joint clicks,
From the driver's wheels on Thirty-six.
Each chug throws white clouds about—
We're leaving Town; we're pulling out!
And two young boys, Bob and Frank, breathe deep and squeal,
From the keen excitement which they feel—
The platform moves; the crowd glides past;
Ed Hoskins waves; we're moving fast!
Greensboro goes—we're off at last;
Smooth riding—soon we hit the curve,
An easy jar, a gentle swerve.
Through the window, puffing in the lead,
We see the monster boost our speed.
O'er Market Street our engine moves,
O'er traffic coming down its grooves;
Past Summit Street, by Fisher Park,
By woodsy branches, cold and dark—
There Church Street for a flash is spied,
Along the Railroad's western side—
Its sidewalk where 'neath summer's sky,
We stand to watch the trains go by.
Another swerve, the throttle's shut;
We're coasting fast into the cut.
A bank jumps 'cross the windowpane;
We look for further sights in vain—
Inside, we dare not move or stir;
Outside, there's just a moving blur.
Wild wonder as we contemplate,
We wish to go investigate—
But soon faint specks of view appear,

And we see 'mid flashing flicks and frills
Small houses of the White Oak Mills;
We dash on fast above the ground—
There's a far-off lake; the view's profound.
Soft hills in green rise all around,
Then a deadly roar, a deafening state:
An atom blast with all its weight,
The crash sound of a passing freight,
The boys (Bob and Frank) each grab a parent's arm
To shield themselves from sudden harm—
They grab and clutch with great alarm!
But the roaring avalanche moves fast,
And quick as it came, the peril's past,
Straight southward on its speedy run,
On the outer track from Washington;
And farms appear, then farms are gone,
And time moves fast, and we move on;
Then a neck jerk, a coach quiver,
And we rush loudly across Haw River;
And soon to the left, so far off still,
Those distant dots are Reidsville:
This Reidsville that each child likes,
Reidsville, the home of Lucky Strikes.
First, houses, then the stores fly past;
The stretch to the station is reached at last.
Though we brake and we blow, our speed is still fast—
Now Westinghouse grabs with a crushing grip;
We alight at the station and end the trip.

We leave the coach; the train pulls out—
We watch it go, then look about,
And ask an old man standing near,
"Where is the Hotel Belvedere?"
He cites wood stairs and walking feet,
Dropping westwardly to Main Street;
We go down to Main, with hungry intent,
Up by the Confederate Monument,

And see that tribute grand and high,
To a valor that can never die.
(Flash Rebel Raids of Stuart we see,
And "Stonewall" Jackson, and Robert E. Lee.)
Yet four blocks south on Main we dwell,
Then two blocks west to the great Hotel—
And now at long last we are here,
In the turning door at the Belvedere;
The boys dash for the magazines,
And soon devour the picture scenes,
As they grab and read the comics,
Which they dramatize with mimics.
But soon they fret on empty stomachs,
And since we've all grown weak and thinner,
We quickly wash and fix for dinner.

Those savory foods dispel the gloom,
As we walk into the Dining Room,
A Happy Crowd, a jovial whirl,
Like people in another World.
By many ways from far and near,
Folks gather thus, throughout the year;
Look for a friend—he may be here,
Relaxing at the Belvedere—
And quite hearty, as all strong folk should,
On food 'twould make the Gods feel good;
Each dish a pick-up and a cheer,
The happy hour, the Belvedere—

And all the family feels sublime,
The prospect's for a long, long time.

Mortal You

You are now fighting on the Time Front;
Many dangerous tales you have to tell of battles.
Often you have been wounded on the front line,
And have had close calls with death.
From automobiles, disease, illness, wars, accidents,
Personal encounters and other violence,
You have so far escaped.
You have won countless battles against Time;
From hard-fought fields you have always emerged.
Often you have been heroic,
For those who have lived for many years in this world
Have all been heroes, many times;
You have had few furloughs
And have survived under great difficulties and entrenched hardships,
Because you have had what it takes, and it takes much.

Your final epitaph could read,
"Here lies 'Mortal You,' died———, a veteran of the Time War
On Planet Earth,
Justly entitled to the Croix de Guerre,
Killed in action.
He miraculously survived all battles but the last."

Higher Law

On you we all rest,
As trees upon roots,
Your use by man
Raises man above brutes.

But higher and better
Help the law grow—
The criminal and civil—
And the "Sermon on the Mount" kind.

Up and up we must rise
As with leaven,
Many times higher,
More than seven times seven.
'Til the Higher Law leads into Heaven,
Higher and higher let us climb and plod,
'Til the Higher Law merges with God.

Westward Friendly, Ho!

Westward from East Market Street Turn-off, in Greensboro, North Carolina,
Our car moves down famed Friendly Avenue, a one-way rolling road,
As we glide through open spaces, on a segment new and wide,
Four lanes of restless traffic, cars running side by side.
Soon there's a dash 'neath a large white bridge
(Southern Railway's Main Tracks),
And then a sweep across lowlands and over a creek
To Forbis Street, and then a climb up to Davie,
At last to Big Business on Elm, where we stop for the light.

Crossing Elm between tall buildings, we drop down
Past City Hall and the Library and West Market Church
To "Commerce Bottom,"
Then climb a rolling hill by the Federal Building,
Only to ease down again past Sear's Store and Grace Methodist Church,
On a gentle rolling loop of this great Piedmont Roller Coaster.
We roll on down between large homes and yards and high oak trees
With brightly colored leaves falling in the Autumn Foliage—
Sunlight, like Ancient Athens had—
A cloud-specked sky, the blue of Heaven above—
"Carolina, Carolina, Heaven's Blessings attend her;
While we live, we will cherish, protect and defend her."

Rolling in the blaze of Autumn, over the loops—
Down to Edgeworth Street and up to Spring, down to Cedar,
Arching like a long rainbow over Cromwell Bridge,
And then dropping down again to Wilson,

Then rising sharply to Mendenhall
And on up by the huge First Baptist Church, to the top of the ridge.

And from here, on ahead, over a distant, dazzling hilltop,
We see cars quietly disappearing in the sunlight's western glow,
As we follow in the flow.
What a good way to go,
Westward Friendly, Ho!

Spring from the Southeastern Building

Spring is here.
A Heavenly sunlight, such as ancient Athens had,
Floats through the out-of-doors,
And a green growth takes the Earth.

In the distance at Proximity, Revolution and White Oak Mills,
Tall stacks, though miles apart,
Grow through the green to form a huge triangle,
Bigger at this end, but silhouetted against the earth and sky
Near the horizon, and staked out prominent in the sun.

Far off, from a White Oak spire, soft smoke slowly rises;
Many large water tanks and buildings loom above the foliage.
In the distance, there's the great Moses Cone Hospital,
And nearer by, among the rest, I see my large old White House,

On Smith Street, shining with a comfortable glow,
And closer still, the relics of old Wesley Long,
And the present Women's "Y"—
All enveloped in the rays of Heaven, which burgeons out
The best from within them—
As they are all bathed by the soft light
And fragrant breath of this clear day of Spring.

The Eastern Regional Tournament

It's the Ides of March, 1968 (March fifteenth);
Two great Yankee Teams: Columbia and Saint Bonaventure,
Have come from New York State here to Raleigh, N.C.
To battle with two N.C. Champions,
Davidson and North Carolina, in this
Eastern Regional National Basketball Tournament.

On this fateful day many years ago,
Said the Soothsayer to Julius Caesar,
"Beware of the Ides of March!"
And in *Macbeth,* 'twas said,
'Til "Birnam wood to high Dunsinane ... come" [you shall live].
Now it's the Ides of March and
New York to Caroline has come,
But who is to beware?
Comparatively it's the reverse of *Macbeth*—
The City to the Woods has come—
Columbia against Davidson at seven,
Carolina against Saint Bonaventure at nine,
With the two winners tonight,
Playing each other tomorrow night in the Finals.

At the start we have four great champions
Flitting on the floor.
But only one can be king
Of this vicious, fateful Ides of March Tournament!
And the Soothsayer, gazing ahead, says,
"Fate for that one shall be kinder,
The winner, North Carolina."

The Mount Airy Train

In the wee of the night, that noise again,
An offkey blast, then a loud refrain,
That robot trudge, that awkward creaky strain,
As it struggles in the same place again and again.
Will it ever arrive in its laboring pain—
That old Mount Airy train?

Fond midnight had slid across my eyes,
As dreamland beckoned—
And then that blow—
Then a pause, then another withering shriek,
Next a rumbling, shaking sound of an engine plodding,
A diesel workhorse thwarted at its chores.

But on it comes, a series of grade crossings start,
Only a hundred yards apart,
And soon twenty blows and blasts to abide,
Which wake up couples a half mile on each side;
They gripe and curse as they strive for slumber,
But soon get active and increase their number,
Their destined fate, a high birth rate,
Intense pain, intense pleasure—all, of course,
From the midnight ploddings of an old iron horse.

On the Way to the Moon

Is the earth erupting? Is all Hell loose?
Through steam clouds, a high tower moves upward, riding a volcano,
Lifted by a raging naked flame that rises with it.
Wherefrom? Whereto? This fiery dragon? This spectral monster?
The fury of the ages hurries with it!

The Moon Landing

A tall tower rises into the heavens.
Three modern Elijahs in a fiery chariot, go up to glory,
Armstrong, Aldrin, and Collins,
But unlike Elijah they will come back to Earth;

A new Babel, movable and powered for conquest, is on its way,
Spaceship of the Ages—sky eater, moon-bound missile,
Destined to open up new worlds and new thinking,
To take the lid off of stagnated concepts and bring into view
A truer look at the Infinite and a freer use of
Thought, observation, and experimentation for all peoples.

Those Interplanetary Men

First humans to ever step on foreign soil,
Space conquerors, brothers of the cosmos,
Galavanting in the sunlight on the moon,
Until they were footsore with moon dust,
Earth's representatives in the Cosmos,
You and your project have proved that man's capacity is infinite.

The Descent to the Moon

They're in their tiny module,
Just released from the bigger craft,
All on their own, dropping down into strange new country.
There it is, twenty-six miles below.
Soon they approach the ten-mile altitude,
The point of no return.
The instruments read, "satisfactorily."

The commander, Armstrong, talks to space control
And gets the green light and continues dropping.
Soon they see a giant crater.
They are dropping toward its center.
The fuel is dangerously low,
And the huge-mouthed crater's aglow.

Armstrong, his heart pounding one hundred fifty-six beats a minute,
Takes over the manual controls and turns sharply
And flies a mile or so to smooth ground,
A skillful sidewise module thrust,
Then lands softly in the lunar dust—

Armstrong and Aldrin, the first humans
To ever land on foreign soil.

The Candidate for the Senate

When others tried to beat him in,
His strength became the strength of ten;
For every post he's ever vied,
He's undefeated and untied;
Great former Governor, North State's pride,
Fit to stand by Raleigh's side,
He's helped the masses, led their fights,
And is champion of the people's rights.
His program gave the State a lift,
All-purpose roads, good schools, and thrift,
And not the least among his graces,
He cleaned graft from higher places,
Put 'lectric power in rural places,
And left our great State strong and free,
When his term expired in Fifty-three.

There's a race on for the Senate;
Do the people want him in it?

But first there's one thing, let us note—
An appointee serves without our vote;
A change in status is expected,
For him who serves, but's not elected;

Call Scott and plead with voices stout;
Your sentiments should bring him out.
Entice him from his fertile farm,
And make the welcome loud and warm,
As the masses shout the great alarm;
Back Scott, the people's North State Pride—
He's undefeated and untied.
Once in the race, he'll fight and win it,
And add new luster to the Senate;
For you and me, he'll do a lot,
The people's choice, our friend, Kerr Scott.

Easter

Behold the radiant Sunday Sun,
And Lilies white on Easter Morn;
All flowers arrayed in bloom and glow,
Great Nature's pride—her cosmic show,
A greenish carpet gilds the land,
And stirs the pulse of every man.

Just yesterday 'twas wet and dark
With fitful whips of wind and rain,
As though there'd ne'er be sun again.
At last the storm grew tired and worn—
Then left our Earth sore, drenched, and torn.

But now, a calm, clear day is here,
The most beautiful in all the year;
On this day let great thoughts be born,
Behold the radiant Sunday Sun,
And Lilies white on Easter Morn.

Unite

Unite, you nations of the world;
Not for long can you stand alone.
A chaotic stillness grips the earth;
Death's in your dial tone.

We could all unite and transform the world—
A Utopia for the whole human race,
To as fair a globe as orbits its sun,
In the limits of infinite space.

Too long, seeds of defeat, we've sown,
Such as hopelessness, hate, and fear,
And a negative harvest of death and despair,
Is gathered in, at the close of each year.

Unite all peoples of the earth;
STOP WAR and its endless strife—
One for all and all for one,
The United Nations Way of life.

Our United Nations*

Our United Nations—how great and how grand!
World Home for all peoples,
The Parliament of Man!
World Peace and World Progress,
Should thrive under your dome;
Federation of Nations,
A new life has dawned.†

World Assemblies of the Nations—cause improvements to flower,
Bills of Rights for all people,
Responsibilities for all,
Strong protection for the whole world,
Like the springtime's sweet breath,
Will bring Blessings of Good Life,
In place of mass death.

Great love for all earth's people, spelled out in world law,
United by Charter,
For defense and great growth,
World Opinion make the U.N.
Grow in wisdom and force,
A millennium for all men,
Should be on its course.

Heaven help man's greatest venture, world peace through world law,
Growing hope for all peoples
On this mammoth globe;
Nations thus linked together,
World salvation can give—
Our United Nations,
Eternally live!

---

*Sing to the tune of "Flow Gently, Sweet Afton."
†Repeat verse 1 for the final verse.

Bob Fitzsimmons

When nine years old, he and his family,
Embarked from Helston, Cornwall, England, for New Zealand.
Five thousand miles of water lay before this Cornish Family,
And three months of sailing on the trackless oceans was required;
Twice in raging storms, they almost sank at sea,
But struggling gamely on, at last they floundered into port
And docked at Littleton, New Zealand—
Poor immigrants in a strange new world.

And before many years, he, a redhead, spindly legged, lanky lad,
In spite of tender years, must soon hire out,
Apprentice helper in a blacksmith's shop.
He did his master's bidding.
From morn to night, he tread the smoky, grueling grind,
Fetched shoes and nails and cutting blades,
Helped hold and pacify the horses,
And did many chores about the shop.

And, as he got his growth, he turned the bellows' crank—
It ground out smoke, and quickly made the forge and horseshoes
    super hot,
And soon, with gloves and apron on,
And tongs to hold each horseshoe, up, upon the anvil,
He swung his smithy's hammer, like the norse God, Thor,
And flexed his growing arms and shoulders,
As he molded the hot horseshoes,
With artistic precision, to fit,
Each waiting beast of burden.

Then with the horse's hoof upturned,
He nailed each shoe on, and smoothed it up—
This lanky lad, young, ruddy Bob Fitzsimmons.

At eighteen years of age, he flexed his muscles at a boxing contest—
Weighing only one hundred forty pounds, he fought the heavies,
And knocked out four of them one night,
To become the Champion of New Zealand.
Next year, he knocked out the Maori Giant, Slade,
And four more, to win again.

He later lived in New South Wales and Australia,
As a horseshoeing smith, who also boxed.
In time, he whipped all comers
In New Zealand and Australia, except Jim Hall;
And years later, at twenty-eight, taking passage, he arrived one day,
So far away: on the western coast of the U.S.A.
And he was still a smith, and he still was fighting.
When he fought, he amazed with his ability to KO with either hand.

After years in America, he fought the Pro Middleweight,
Jack Dempsey, the famous nonpareil, and
Won in the thirteenth round to become
The Middleweight Champion of the world.

Soon he fought the Pro Heavyweights.
He chilled Joe Choynski and the giant, Maher,
And then was later signed to fight the Pro Heavy Champ, Jim Corbett.

On St. Patrick's Day in '97, for conquest or for pity,
There came into an outdoor Nevada Ring, set up at Carson City,
A tall, balding, wide-shouldered, six-foot-one-inch, spindly legged,
Redheaded, freckled-faced, thirty-five-year-old gangling thing,
So odd, so lithe, so weird: just one hundred sixty-seven pounds,

So light in weight to fight the Heavyweight,
Jim Corbett, the Champion, weight, one hundred eighty-five pounds,
Fastest Heavy known to man,
And conqueror of the Great John L. Sullivan—
And Corbett was our first Heavyweight Champion of the whole world.

In the early rounds, Corbett, with his speed and skill,
Scored, and piled up points at will;
Left jabs and lightning blows of Gentleman Jim,
Smeared Fitz with blood and shook him,
A dancing phantom, Corbett—in and out,
A spring against the ropes, then back,
One, two, bam and away.

In the sixth round, a right to the jaw
Sent Fitz thudding to the floor,
But his heroic wife, Rose, jumped up at the ring corner, commanding,
"Cover up and hit him in the slats, Bob."
He arose, groggily at the count of nine, covered up, threw body blows,
And weathered the bloody round.

By the tenth and eleventh he was fighting on even terms,
And soon came the fourteenth, the greatest round of all times:
Corbett danced in for the kill, with his right cocked and head high;
Fitz started a right for Corbett's head, but seeing the head move back,
Switched and shot a quick long left deep into Corbett's solar plexus,
And then, Corbett's fall did begin,
And for Corbett that was the floor, and that was the end.
That closed out this fateful bout;
Jim lay prostrate, as he was counted out.

Soon a roar of applause for the game old man,
As the referee held up Fitz's strong right hand!
Next, an all-night celebration in honor of Bob and Rose,
With "Ole" Carson City Hospitality, including food and drink, followed.

Telegraphs clicked, soon the sports news unfurled,
"A kangaroo punch—new heavy champ of the world."
And this comment,
"That solar-plexus punch that makes 'em all stop;
The taller they come, the harder they drop"—

Preserved in history, proclaimed in ditty,
His solar-plexus punch at Carson City—
Heavy Champ, in spite of his own light weight,
Perhaps the greatest of the great?—
Ruby Bob Fitzsimmons.

The Constitution

For five long years
The thirteen original colonies
Warred against that Empire
On whose domain the sun never set—
A fledgling band against a host of giants,
A foolish try against superhuman odds.
And yet they turned George III's world upside down,
And wrecked his military might at Yorktown.

But they, themselves, were groggy from the fray—
They were too weak to drive his other forces,
Clinton's, later Carleton's, from New York,
Just threatened them for two more years,
Until the British left for good.

But though they won their freedom, after seven years,
They had no general government—
Only discord and petty wars remained—
And thus ensued four years of anarchy, strife, and pandemonium,
Among thirteen pigmy nations,
Each suspicious and jealous of the others.
Virginia and Maryland staged tariff fights,
River brawls, and small border wars!
Why had the Revolutionary War been fought?
The tyranny of George III was supplanted by a worse one!

Then, finally, in desperation, Virginia and Maryland
Arranged a conference at Annapolis,
To work out river and bay rights
For their joint use of the Potomac and Chesapeake,
And invited Pennsylvania and Delaware to come along—
The purpose: to adjust commercial matters
Which all four had in common—
But bold Virginia, ignoring the limited purpose,
Suggested a General Convention.

The first Convention met at Annapolis in September 1786,
But only five States came: New York, New Jersey,
Pennsylvania, Delaware, and Virginia.
However, Alexander Hamilton, saving the day,
Made a written report of the Convention to the legislatures
Of those five States and also to Congress,
Calling to attention that: "New Jersey delegates had been authorized
To consider commercial matters, and other important matters
Necessary to the common interests
And permanent harmony of the several states,"
And suggested calling another Convention
With enlarged powers to meet at Philadelphia,
"Because the power of regulating trade
Is of such comprehensive extent,
That to adjust it will require
Adjusting other parts of the Federal System."

Congress acted, and, on February 21, 1787,
With eleven states present, it resolved,
That "such a Convention appeared to be the most probable means
Of establishing in these States a firm national government,"
And that it considered it "expedient" that such a Convention
Be held in May 1787, at Philadelphia, "for the sole and express purpose
Of revising the Articles of Confederation
And reporting to the Congress, and the several legislatures,
Such alterations and provisions therein,
As shall, when agreed to in Congress,
And confirmed by the States,
Render the Federal Constitution
Adequate to the exigencies of government—
And the preservation of the Union."

The legislatures of twelve states (all except Rhode Island),
Appointed deputies to the Constitutional Convention;
Fifty-five delegates attended;
Thirty-four were lawyers;
Forty-six had served in state legislatures;
Forty-two had been delegates to the Continental Congress;
Eight had signed the Declaration of Independence,
And six the Articles of Confederation.

Delegates came from far and wide,
Filled with freedom and state's pride.
The first meeting was held at Independence Hall
On May twenty-fifth, seventeen and eighty-seven, and
George Washington was elected chairman.

Soon Edmund Randolph introduced the Virginia Plan,
Drafted by James Madison and supported by Wilson and King,
Setting up an Executive and a Judiciary and a Council of Revision,
With a lower house, based on population,
The lower house to elect the upper, etc.;
And then Charles Pinckney of South Carolina
Introduced a plan similar to Virginia's.
Then followed thirteen meetings in committee
Upon the Virginia Plan.
Then in June, seventeen and eighty-seven, Paterson, of New Jersey,
Introduced his plan,
Giving Congress the power to regulate foreign and interstate commerce,
And calling for a plural executive, and a federal judiciary,
And providing for a dual government:
Namely, national control over state laws and actions,
To a limited degree only,

And with states otherwise supreme in their domain,
And making the Acts of Congress and the Treaties with nations,
And the Constitution itself,
The Supreme Law of the land,
And also providing for an equal vote by each state
In the National Congress (this appealed to the small states only)—
And so raged the battle between the large and the small states,
For another month—

Then in July, seventeen and eighty-seven,
Was adopted the great compromise, suggested by Dickinson of
  Delaware, and,
Urged by the delegates from Connecticut—Sherman, Ellsworth, and
  Johnson,
Providing that the number of each state's
Representatives in the lower house,
Be based on its population, with a minimum of one,
But in the upper house, allotting to each state,
Regardless of size or population, two Senators.
  Sherman, Gerry, Davie, Morris, Franklin, Williamson, and others
  encouraged the compromise.
And then, the Convention selected a Committee of Detail:
Rutledge, *Wilson,* Randolph, Ellsworth, and Gorham—
To rough-draft the Constitution;
And thereafter a Committee of Style:
Johnson, *Morris,* Madison, King, and Hamilton—
To arrange and refine it in final form.
And then with slight changes it was approved by the full Convention.
Ratification of, and Amendments to, the Constitution
Were provided for by a vote of Congress and by State Conventions
Especially chosen by the people in each state;
And ratification by nine states was adjudged sufficient,
For those ratifying—
To form a government.

An executive elected by the people for four years,
Each Congressman for two, and each Senator for six,
And a Supreme Court, the members of which
Were to be appointed by the President for life,
Were finally agreed upon.
And the Constitution was duly signed by thirty-nine delegates,
On September seventeenth, seventeen and eighty-seven.
On September twenty-eighth, seventeen and eighty-seven,
With eleven states present,
Congress unanimously approved transmission
Of it, to the State Legislatures,
For submission to State Conventions, for approval—
And on December seventh, seventeen and eighty-seven,
Delaware was the first to ratify, and then followed
Pennsylvania, New Jersey, Georgia, Connecticut,
Massachusetts, Maryland, South Carolina,
New Hampshire, Virginia, New York,
North Carolina, and Rhode Island.

The great Washington was later chosen by
The Electors, our first President, and John Adams, Vice President,
And thus was born the greatest Governmental Plan ever designed by man;
That dual system of government:
The Federal Government supreme in its limited domain,
The respective States in theirs,
And all unspecified powers being left,
To the States or to the People.
Both Federal and State Governments had three divisions:
Executive, Legislative, and Judicial,
Which were checks and balances on each other,
Governments, of the People, by the People, for the People,
A new nation, a new concept, a new dawn for man!
Created by the great Constitution of the United States of America.

And a few years later, encouraged by Jefferson and others, in
    seventeen ninety-one,
There were added the First Ten Amendments:
The Great Bill of Rights.

And, in 1803, there was established by a decision of the Supreme
    Court
(*Marberry* v. *Madison*),
That new dimension, invention, and prerogative in Democratic
    Government:
The power by the Supreme Court of the United States,
To construe and interpret the constitutionality of laws—
Including even the power to declare a law unconstitutional.
Thereby keeping Congress within the bounds designated by the
    Constitution
And insuring its conformance to the rules.

Surely, this was the greatest document ever drawn by man,
Delineating the finest system ever created.
Truly, the delegates, goaded by the necessity to survive,
And blest by Heaven, in the noblest undertaking of man,
In four months of arduous toil,
Accomplished the impossible, achieved immortality,
And brought about the just principles and pattern for practical
    democratic government,
For the United States and mankind:
Cast out the weak, installed the strong,
Forsook the false, brought in the true,
Built even better than they knew,
There at Philadelphia.

Old Pomona Street Line at Greensboro

A dip in the past, the clang of iron I hear,
Those streetcar rides of yesteryear;
The horsecar flourished 'til 1901.
When electric trolley cars started to run;
Then a sizable collection of long urban lines
Was built through the city like an arbor of vines.

From the old Southern station with its smoke and flare
There were two tracks up Elm to the Courthouse Square;
On the high court tower, like the sides of a block,
Were four giant faces of the Courthouse clock;
At the Square, cars came up, at each quarter hour,
With bells ringing, switches banging, and that overhead power.

And here, a left quarter turn of one track to the west,
Was the route that most people considered the best;
In riding this line there were many privileges—
It was scenic and wound by two girls' colleges.

From the Square due west, a half mile downgrade,
Then across an old Railroad,
Then up a high hill by Greensboro(Female) College,
And thence on west to the Tate Street curve,
Thence south with Tate, a half mile to Spring Garden,
Thence west on Spring Garden by the Normal College,
Yet two miles on west, by Lindley Park Pond,
Thence a mile west through dense woods, to the end at Pomona—
Four miles of beauty, gardens, and privileges,
And serving the girls of both of the colleges.

Three car switches graced the line, each a famous landmark,
Greensboro College, Kenilworth, and Lindley Park;
Cars passed at Kenilworth at each quarter hour,
With wheels rumbling and motors humming, from that overhead power.

Long, lumbering cars ran from six (A.M.) to eleven (P.M.),
Seventy-five, seventy-six, and old seventy-seven,
And a short car, fifty-four, that rode both bouncy and blinky,
The latest in style—a modern dinkey.

The motormen, often called "Captains," were friendly, glamorous, and kind,
On the old Pomona Streetcar Line;
Each swayed with his trolley car's temperamental swerve,
As it dipped down a straightway, or bumped 'round a curve.

In Spring, how delightful, enchanting, and fine,
To take a car ride on the old Pomona Line;
To see so much so quickly solved a complication,
And the trip by the colleges was quite an education.

There were truck farms, cold springs, and ripe grapes on the vine,
Along the old Pomona Streetcar Line;
There were large homes and green lawns, and flowers divine,
Along the old Pomona Streetcar Line;
And poplars and oak trees with sprinklings of pine,
Along the old Pomona Streetcar Line.

A rock, a shake, a constant jar,
Each lumbering old Pomona car,
And the clank of iron, the yaw, the pitch,
The rhythmical sequence 'cross the switch;

The Public Service Company
Offered to each citizen and resident
Six tickets for a quarter—
Charles B. Hole, President.

Chair car seventy-seven, was heavy, elegant, and fine,
As it lumbered along, on the old Pomona Line;
And to ride "Double Seven," made one cast off his burden—
Double Seven, the famous chair car, of Mister Ike Jerden.

The hand throttle and the air brakes, were mysterious and swanky,
Eight-notch speed on large cars, but nine on each dinkey.

There was a kind old bachelor, who for a widow's heart did pine;
They married and took a round trip, on the old Pomona Line,
And when they got home, the boys staged a big parade,
With horns blowing, bells ringing, and a loud serenade.

John White was strong and handsome, and a "Ladies' Man" quite fine,
As he ran streetcar seventy-six, on the old Pomona Line.

Open summer cars ran in warm weather time,
Packed with femininity—a sight quite sublime,
Red cheeks and curls and squealing college girls,
And fluttered-up dresses and gusty wind whirls.

On past the colleges, and known for miles around,
Was the quaint little settlement of Cooper Town,
With its steepled church, town store, and mill,
Built 'long the railroad, on the ridge of a hill,
Thirteen little houses and as many small lots,
Plain couples and children and cur dogs and pots.

And on Sundays the church steeple rang clear and well,
With that fascinating gift, a train engine's bell;
But in spite of conversions and professions profound,
A little bootleg liquor got stashed underground.

And furniture factories and a planing mill,
Gave work 'cross the railroad from Cooper Town Hill;
The residents reaped the fruits of an active life,
Had a minimum of fist fights and other forms of strife.

And the town, was west of, and I can see it still,
Congressman Kirkpatrick's* spacious home and windmill—also on
    the hill;
And the town, flanked on each side, by a different streetcar track,
Fare—four cents to town to shop, and on the Glenwood line a free
    transfer back;
Wise Reverend Cooper picked a good spot at sight,
Cheap transportation helped a low-budget plight;
And kind Mrs. Cooper, as we were often told,
Helped her husband with the sick, the lame, and the old.
And Cooper Town is due its just priority,
It was Greensboro's first real housing authority.

About midway on the line, was a well-known spot,
A large grocery store run by Hanner and Scott,
Where news was exchanged 'round a potbellied stove,
Of all things here below, and in Heaven above;
"Soon a car rumbles up on its heavy iron rollers,
As the "Captain" rushes in for two Coca-Colas;
He commands their respect, as they greet him with pride;
He goes back to the icebox, as men talk by his side,
Of his forty-mile speed and this new modern ride."
"Hotch" Faires Garage and Yum-Yum Creams were near this stop,
And Jones Store, Hodgin's Meats, and Tuttle's Barber Shop.

Some folks arose early, rather than later,
Dr. Johnson had a large cook, named Vyater,
Who got up before dawn, and started breakfast by six,
As she heard the first car enter the Kenilworth Switch;
But once she aroused the children with smiling delight,
And called them down in their sad sleepy plight,

---

*Hon. Sanford Kirkpatrick was a Civil War veteran and U.S. Congressman fom Iowa, who retired in 1916 and moved to Greensboro. He was called "Bullet Cushion" by the other Congressmen, for he had been frequently wounded when he served as Revenue Officer.

Dorothy, Allen, and Wade,
In a manner that was so guileless and carefree—
For crisp breakfast bacon, eggs, and hot coffee,
But the children stayed so sleepy and no more cars came.
Things were so still and quiet—what could be the blame?
Vyater hadn't risen to the six o'clock switch-entering sound,
But to the midnight clank of the last car to town!

Once there was an incident, around nineteen thirty-five,
When we had a taste of adventure and great excitement came alive.
'Twas near midnight at Pomona, "Captain" Maness felt fine,
As he prepared to head east, on the old Pomona Line;
He pulled the door lever closed, put his hand on the throttle,
Released the air brakes, and started off with a rattle.
He moved out fast and soon approached the Winston Road,
But slowed before he crossed, as required by the Code,

Then threw speed in the dinkey's loose, bouncing joints,
As he ran for the deep woods fast on nine points.
At length, as he passed through dense growth 'long the line,
He reached a sharp "S" curve surrounded by pine,
And was shocked, as he saw with a sudden surprise,
On the track just ahead, a large pile of cross ties!

He threw on the air brakes, then reversed, as he worked like a Turk,
But his fender struck the cross ties, and he stopped with a jerk.
"This is a stick-up! Open up and hand over your money,
Or we'll kill you," said a "Voice" from the night.
"Okay, it's all yours," said Maness, trembling with fright;
Soon he saw a head move from behind a power pole,
A quick shot from his hip, and he drilled that head a hole;
The man dropped in his tracks, like a bounty hunter's goods,
As his cutthroat companion took to the woods.

Next morn at Hanes's Funeral Home,
A certain man was quite dead,
All starched up with rigor mortis
And a hole through his head.

There were callers by the hundreds,
As Hanes greeted most by name,
But with dignity, as if 'twere the Governor,
Or another stricken man of fame.

But once inside at the morgue,
There were whispers apt and able,
From the middle of the big room,
'Round the body, as it lay upon a table:

"What a dead-eye shot was 'Captain' Maness";
About "how much the poor 'Hood' had bled";
That "he got what he deserved:
A light-hole through his head."

Yes, in the old days, the gone days,
Those adventures were divine,
The summer cars, the college girls,
Ripe grapes on the vine.

Streetcars were exciting,
And the service was fine
Along the old Pomona Streetcar Line.

Back in the Good Old Days

Back in the good old days—
Folks had such peculiar ways.
Man had arrived and was proud indeed;
Horse and buggy made the fastest speed.
Travel was tough, but thoughts were pure;
The roads were paved with horse manure,
Back in the good old days.

The housefly was a pirate bold;
He flew up through the privy hole,
Yet higher and higher, with gusto and zoom,
And straight to the mansion dining room,
Back in the good old days!

Life was slow, discreet, and sweet;
Ignorance made it all complete.
Typhoid raged and people died;
Mothers wailed and children cried,
As raiding germs increased their kill.
Some speakers said it was God's Will,
Back in the good old days.

Halloween, on an Old Streetcar

A motorman's life could be rough,
And making a schedule might be tough.
Life on a streetcar got plenty mean,
Soon after dark on Halloween.

Soon the iron tracks became slick,
With a Satan's Manna put on thick,
And then there were troubles along the lines,
Especially on the steep inclines.

One Halloween, young men of a certain neighborhood,
Ever hungry for a thrill,
Slipped out into the dark midnight,
To the steep G.C. Hill.

With wicked intent, they rubbed the steep descent,
With bacon grease and fat;
The last car to town, suddenly went down,
In exactly nothing flat.

"A terrible danger," the old folks said,
"At the bottom was the track of the Mount Airy train;
'Twas an outrageous act of vandalism—'twas insane."

"No danger," the crazy youngsters said. "That poky train? Don't have a fit!
That greased streetcar on Halloween was far too fast for it."

Judge Lon McGraw

No N.C. Judge could charge the law,
More ably than Judge Lon McGraw;
State statutes and reports he read,
And stored them in his shapely head.
His charge flowed clear without a flaw,
Recounting facts, explaining law.
He smoked his pipe; he chewed his cud,
And through his veins flowed serious blood.
A Presbyterian Scot was he,
On crime could use severity;
When sentenced, each defendant squirmed,
On each appeal, 'twas "McGraw affirmed"!

In 'twenty-three 'twas scheduled he should
Try the "Auto-Pirate": Occo Crood,
Notorious Highwayman, tough and bold,
Who'd slugged and killed one Cartlin cold.
Crowds braved the Courtroom's sickening stench,
As His Honor climbed to the Cranford Bench.
Hundreds of men were called to the spot,
Ere twelve were passed and a jury got.

The State's first witness on the stand,
Swore Mister Cartlin was a pawnshop man,
That witness was clerking in the store,
Checking the pawn goods o'er and o'er,
When Occo came with speed and stealth,
To part said Cartlin from his wealth.
Said Cartlin counted the cash he kept,
As closer and closer Occo crept;
A club came down on Cartlin's head,
And two days later he was dead—
Then as Occo fled the scene,
He grabbed his lone hand full of "green."

Quick telling of this story once,
Was not enough for Lawyer Klonts;
"Had you seen Crood before this day?
Yes or No?" The witness said, "No."
"Had he ever been there before this day?
Yes or No?" The witness said, "No."
"Had he pawned a watch there before this day?
Yes or No?" The witness said, "No."
Klonts drew a pawn check from out his desk,
"Is it Crood's?" The witness said, "Yes."
"For a Hampden Watch?" The witness said, "Yes."
"So Crood had been there?" The witness said, "Maybe."
"And asked for his watch?" He didn't know,
Then turned white, as he looked quite humble.
Was he slightly wrong? Will the State take a tumble?

Crood went on the stand and told of the pawn,
Said he tendered the money required to redeem,
His rebuff, his curses, his blow on the head,
Denied he got cash, admitted he fled,
Admitted all crimes the Solicitor read.
With further evidence produced and resisted,
The State concluded and both sides rested.

The Judge rapped the Bench from his lofty place:
"Defendant's Counsel may argue his case."

Klonts' speech to the Jury was loud and gruff;
He pulled no punches, but raised the roof:
"Is this cold-blooded murder? Where, Gentlemen, where?
For a manslaughter job, shall he sit in the Chair?"
But Solicitor Sprule yelled, raised his fist and his knee,
"A clear case of murder in the first degree."

Ten minutes elapsed from the speech-making fury,
Ere the Judge began his Charge to the Jury:
"Gentlemen of the Jury, in the Bill of Indictment
Occo Crood is charged with the murder of one Mr. Cartlin;
He pleads not guilty to said charge of murder.

A murder which shall be perpetrated by means of lying in wait,
Or by any other kind of deliberate and premeditated killing,
Or which is committed in the perpetration of any robbery,
Or the attempt to perpetrate any robbery or felony,
Shall be deemed to be murder in the first degree.
All other kinds of murder shall be deemed to be
Murder in the second degree. Manslaughter is the
Felonious killing of another without premeditation or malice"—
And thus on and on for two full hours.

Was it death in the Chair, or Prison to be?
The Twelve found Crood guilty of second degree.
The punishment set for this crime foul and dirty:
"Not less than two years and not more than thirty."

Some thought the sentence could perhaps be foreseen—
"May be around two years, or as much as fourteen?
Or may be, about halfway between?"

But soon the Judge said, "Stand up, Crood."
His Honor looked at Crood long and hard,
"You, who hate the laws of man and God"—
Then continuing 'midst chews and tears,
"The sentence of the Court is thirty years
In the State's Prison at Raleigh, North Carolina,
At hard labor, prisoner to wear stripes—
He's in your custody, Mister Sheriff."

Decades have flown as time has crept on;
It's many a day that His Honor's been gone.
Peace to His Soul, Renown to His Clay—
We miss him since he went away.
His Grave, in Green Lawn's Hallowed Ground—
The Crime Rate improved when he served in Town.

Snow Blizzard

It's March the ninth, 1960—the blizzard's on.
From my office on Elm (at 119 North Elm Street), I look southward,
Past the square where Market (Street) crosses—
It's daytime and eleven o'clock A.M.

Now the air is white with falling snowflakes and snow flurries—
And all quite blinding as they fall—
The neon lights along the "Drag" are on,
And dimly pierce the visibility,
And cause an odd, retiring effect.

Lighted cars, trucks, and buses move straight toward me up one-way Elm;
Soon they all halt suddenly at the Square
Before that Deity, the Stop light, as a burly policeman stands near—
Soon it changes and the east- and west-bound cars on Market
Seize the intersection and burst across the Square two hundred feet away.

A black janitor wearing leggings and with a toboggan on,
Throws salt from a large can he carries,
In front of Vanstory's and the N.C. Bank;
He finishes, turns up the can and shakes it,
As strong winds gust around the building and whip his face with snow.

He goes back inside for more salt.
Five inches have fallen since day,
And yet there's no letup;
Two women with raised umbrellas cross at Market,
As the snow keeps piling up;
Most pedestrians have tired, chilled, and gone home,
In surrender to this sudden invasion.

Is Canada to Greensboro come?
Or is this the "Blitzkrieg" of a new Ice Age,
Showing with "Hitlerian" suddenness?

All the while, above the Elm and Market Junction,
The tall spires of Julian Price's Jefferson Standard Life Insurance
   Building,
Are lost, as they rise into the sky—
The face of Charlie Wimbish's Big Clock on the northeast corner
   (to my left),
Is now fading under a white cloud,
And the show window at Belk's Store, on the southeast corner,
With its female models and large dolls,
Appears grotesque and unreal through the haze.

Numerous parked cars along the "Drag,"
Have now become white mounds,
Completely snowbound in the storm—
For time has marched on,
And it is now five o'clock and nearly a foot has fallen!

What kind of a day is March 9, 1960?
A day unlike other days,
For the Arctic Storms have blown across Dixie,
And congealed, befuddled, and frozen Greensburghers cold,
And plowed them under a cap of Polar Ice and Snow,
And you are here.

Two-Way Elm

Upon the inner loop, the cars race 'round,
To dodge those long jams of the town,
Which are on Elm Street (our Main Street).
But the cross streets are not all clogged,
And looking down Elm from my window
I see five cross streets,
On which traffic fairly breezes across Elm
In opposite directions, as cars pass each other, in the intersections.

But Elm's a two-way, slow and cluttered drag,
Just a long traffic jungle for a half mile,
At every block a red light and a "depot" wait;
But Elm has fascinations—
At many intersections you can turn off, if you want to,
And if not, there are many stores and displays,
And windows with tempting merchandise and sexy models.
To see them well, you must slow down,
Or stop, so you can look longer.

Of course, the street lights on Elm do stop you all right—
But not just where you want them to;
But you'll, at least, see something from where you stop,
And may greet a friend or so who passes near.
The merchants wanted it slow.

For fifteen years (1950 through 1965),
We had a one-way Elm.
But then cars passed too fast for girls (young and younger),
To study windows,
And trade migrated to the suburbs in bulk lots.
Downtown stores have tried to counterattack.

The City Council has made Elm's forward progress
As slow as horse-and-buggy traffic,
So why not now install lunch and drink counters
By our car windows, and have curb service,
While we wait at each intersection,
As the remaining stores move to the suburbs?

Early Spring

Gone is the north wind's killing blow,
Rough winter's hooks of ice and snow,
And now a mildness fills the air;
A Guilford grandeur's everywhere.
On sunny hilltops robins sing;
Comes soon the fullness of the spring.

A Great World Christmas Tree

The shades of a cold December night come down,
Upon our Town and its environs around;
But silver water tanks at their great height,
Yet reflect the sun's light;
And huge smokestacks, round and lonely,
High above the horizon are lighted dimly.
Yonder smoke, above a far-off (Cone) mill stack, hovers lazily,
While that from the nearby (O'Henry) hotel spire, puffs crazily.
And all the while night spreads and silhouettes itself against
The western sky.

Now red globes, in a line to the top of
The seven-hundred-and-fifty-foot T.V. Tower begin blinking;
And in the distance, through the trees, see the white, red, and green
    lights twinkling,
And red-and-white neon systems, like far-off toys at super marts,
And car lots, begin blaring and glaring;
And twenty minutes later, as crowds hurry below, I notice
Galaxies along Main Street, flaming, fluttering, and flashing.
From this sixth floor, I see that the dark invasion is thorough,
And night has now settled on the round earth, here and about
    Greensboro;

But shining up from the surface of the Earth's blackness,
And fluttering and twinkling with exactness,
Thousands of green, yellow, red, white, and blended lights, I see,
In this Yuletide Glee!
And Lo! Our Town's a tiny segment of a great World Christmas
    Tree!

That Day

A kind neighbor, sensing what was about to be,
Took my young brother and me,
Off for a ride in the country,
And on out to his uncle's rural home;
They let us out that day in May,
To play among the young peach trees—
But an awful pall hung over my head,
An inescapable, terrible dread—
Down each row we walked,
Up each tree we climbed,
And 'twould never leave—
In an hour, he cranked and took us back,
In that old-time Ford—
But still that ever-present dread,
That awful thought was there in my head.

As we reached our home,
Many folks were about—
And a stillness hung in the Sunday air,
And most of our friends and neighbors were there—
And a dreadful sadness was everywhere.

We crept in the back and asked, "How's Marjorie?"
And Mother, fighting tears, said, "All right."
But then she broke and said, "God took her for his own"—
And then put her arms around us, and we all three cried—
The saddest day I ever lived was the day that Marjorie died.

And soon Fred, who was only five,
Asked, "Where is she?"
And Mother said, "They have taken her uptown,
But will bring her back before long,
And you can see her again"—

And then broke into a complete cry all over—
And many neighbors came in to ease us,
And cooked supper for us;
But we couldn't eat—an ever-present weight hung over us,
And Daddy was sick upstairs on the sleeping porch,
And he cried too, when we went up there.

That night they brought her back,
And placed her in the parlor—
In the Southeast corner of the room—
And then they took us in
Where she lay in the little white casket,
Still and white with a head of lovely curls,
Angelic, beautiful, and cold,
Only two and a half years old.

And I stood and looked at her,
And wished many times that I could bring her back,
Or else die myself—
For death would have been a great relief.
And soon, Mrs. Angle came over and put her arm about me,
And said, "Wouldn't you like to kiss Little Sister good-bye?"
But I couldn't move—only froze;
And Mrs. Freeman came from across the road,
And cut a lock of her curly hair for Mother,
And the Johnsons, Forneys, Burns, Smiths, Scotts, Pattersons
College People, and students from the college class of which she was mascot,
Brought flowers and other things,
And all of the neighbors were crying—
And it seemed that everything had come to an end.

Next day her funeral in the house,
Was the saddest I ever saw—
Everyone was weeping and helpless.

And as her procession moved that last two miles,
To the fresh plot in Green Hill Cemetery,
Through our tears, we may have felt strangely close to Heaven.
But when the service at the grave was finished,
I feared Mother would also die,
As we left Marjorie there forever.

Soon after Marjorie was buried,
Mother in spite of her poverty
Designed and had placed at the grave,
A handsome white stone statue of
A little girl with wings—an Angel—
And on it, the inscription,
"A lovely flower so fair, so sweet—
God took her for his own"—
The saddest time I ever lived was the time that Marjorie died.

Spaceman John Glenn's Ride*

They pulled back the gantry,
At Cape Canaveral,
Leaving John Glenn ready for the ride;
Soon the huge missile fired,
A hundred miles into the heavens,
And he went into an orbit glide.

He sped east above the ocean,
Seventeen thousand miles an hour,
And soon the day was gone;
He had a pitch black ride
On to Perth, Australia,
Where the people turned their lights all on.

*Sing to the tune of "The Wreck of the Old 97."

He went 'round the earth,
In ninety-four minutes,
And then circled two times more,
Over Africa, Australia,
And the three big oceans,
Saw wonders never seen before.

He was approaching California,
When his "retros" fired,
And he dropped in our air's upper rim;
He burst 'cross our continent,
In a ball of fire,
But his shield kept the heat from him.

He reached the South Atlantic (Ocean),
Where his parachute was spotted,
By our Western Atlantic Recovery Fleet;
He had a happy splashdown,
Was picked up by the *Noa,*
To make a daring trip complete.

And all the Earth's people,
Acclaimed him gladly,
President Kennedy and folks from every walk;
He had street parades,
In New York and D.C.,
And Congress had him in to talk.

The free world thrills,
To our daring spacemen,
Although it's often perplexed;
The sky's our ocean,
And we'll sail upon it—
Soon the Moon, then Mars is next.

Washington and Lee*

In the distant past, a small school in the valley,
Got helping hands from Washington, then Lee—
At last, became a famous University,
That thrived on work and kept its thinking free.

Surrounded by the azure blue of mountains,
And lofty peaks, far reaching toward the sky,
Here, history drips a fragrance on the present
For all the human family passing by.

Her boys have learned the secrets of achievement,
Have risen through the daily grind and strife;
They now include a host of national leaders,
Outstanding in the varied walks of life.

I liked those ancient mountains of Virginia,
And student days at Washington and Lee;
Recollections may have faded in the distance,
But many, still, are strong and clear to me.

Curved walk and spacious lawn before the Chapel,
A touch of Heaven for those who chance to see,
A kinship flows from these two great immortals,
To all the sons of Washington and Lee.

---

*Sing to the tune of "Little Bright Eyes."

Virginia*

The English founded Jamestown in sixteen and seven,
Their first permanent Colony in the newfound western world;
Soon the Cavalier lived his bold frontier life,
Fought Indians, curbed kings, and knew incessant strife.

Deeply we feel for the Old Dominion,
Dripping in history from the first Colonial days;
There at early Williamsburg, near Jamestown, Virginia,
Came forth Founding Fathers of these United States.

Virginians loomed large in each Continental Congress,
Convened at Philadelphia, where the United States was born.
Richard Henry Lee moved the House for separation;
Young Thomas Jefferson penned the words that set us free.

Hers were Peyton Randolph and bold Patrick Henry,
George Washington, George Mason, and Light-Horse Harry Lee;
Hers was the final field where the British were struck down,
Sweetest gem in history—the victory at Yorktown.

She pioneered for freedom—led the long fight with Britain,
Was a power at Philadelphia when the Constitution was born;
She gave us four great Presidents in the long, long ago;
Washington, Jefferson, Madison, and Monroe.

Rich in major Battlegrounds, the soil of Old Virginia,
Colonial, Revolutionary, and the War between the States,
Resting place of heroes who struggled for each cause,
Raised in moral stature when slavery was overthrown.

---

*Sing to the tune of "Carry Me Back to Ole Virginny."

Free, efficient rule, has been the trend in Old Virginia,
Chief Justice Marshall looms among her greatest sons.
Milestones for freedom, glow bright in her past plights;
Destiny beckons, "Embrace the pending fights."

Deeply we feel for the Old Dominion,
Dripping in history from the first Colonial days;
There at early Williamsburg, near Jamestown, Virginia,
Oft came Founding Fathers of these United States.

The 1952 Presidential Race and Former Races

Hoover was a world-famous man,
His earned wealth a proud possession,
But while he served as president,
We drew the Great Depression.

A crash without much warning call,
Soft Autumn filled the sky,
Inflation soared: the Bubble burst, then,
The piercing panic cry!

Machinery quit; our pay all stopped—
Big Banks devoured our "scrapings."
Foreclosure Traps worked day and night,
And caught our homes and savings.

Soon boxcars crawled with human freight,
Lean Tourists drained of joy;
Some rich, smug in their great estates,
Bedubbed 'em "Hoi Polloi."

The autos vanished from our roads;
The farmer fell apart.
He fused car wreckage with his mule,
And got the "Hoover Cart."

Where could our people turn for help?
Who'd save us from this doom?
From empty stomachs, foreclosed homes,
From Bankruptcy and the tomb?

A statesman high up the Hudson,
Enraged at the people's plight—
"There's nothing to fear but fear itself—
Take heart, take courage, let's fight."

That Democrat, the people's friend,
A people's program built;
The masses came into their own,
With Franklin Roosevelt.

The NRA, the FHA,
Old Age and Bank Security,
A living wage and Farm Relief,
For all a great futurity.

Soon idle wheels began to turn;
Our pockets took on pay.
A great economy reworked,
Moved to a better day.

With Roosevelt, we soon lived well,
And when death struck—a new man
Pushed onward with a people's plan,
The Fighting Harry Truman.

And now the times are booming well;
Employment's at its peak.
The Presidential Term rolls 'round,
And the Great Conventions speak.

The Democrats at Chicago,
Chose Stevenson and Sparkman;
The GOP, a fortnight 'fore,
Picked Eisenhower and Nixon.

The pace is fast—the Die is cast;
The Rubicon's no bother.
Caesar-like, our General Ike,
Wants the governmental toga.

Eisenhower's a great general;
He's clearly reached the top.
But if we make him President,
Will our progress slow and stop?

Hour by hour said Eisenhower
Shows e'er a fondness hearty,
To hobnob with the corporate heads,
The core of the rich-man's party.

Against the New and Fair Deals,
He rants with strong commotions;
Recall 'twas under both Deals,
He won his great promotions.

Why kill the New and Fair Deals,
For a say-nothing, do-nothing plan,
And permit a Business standstill,
That might flatten the common man?

Now each Camp moves its forces up,
In its own style and way—
First Tuesday, come November next,
Is Fall Election Day.

The Democrats with Stevenson,
Bivouac with his own plan,
Can they win the fight and prolong their stay,
Or will Eisenhower be the man?

Peter Francisco and Guilford Courthouse

And there was General Washington,
Reviewing from his horse,
A New York Camp, six thousand drilled—
They knew who was the Boss.

He'd given "Pete" a new forged sword—
So long and great in weight—
For "Pete" was quite an o'ersized lad;
His height was six feet eight.

On hard-fought fields at Brandywine,
Monmouth, and Germantown,
"Aggressive Pete" had won renown,
From Washington on down.

The more men griped, the more they drilled;
Their Sergeant's name was Hollis:
"I'll treat you rough; I'll make you tough—
You've got to beat Cornwallis."

They made Pete tough, they made him smart,
They made him fighting mean.
His enlistment ran out, but he rejoined in the South,
Soon to soldier-boy for Greene.

In muck and mire, his bath of fire,
Was had with Gates at Camden;
He shouldered a cannon, saved it and his Colonel,
But most of the men went running.

When Greene took o'er, 'twas route no more;
He retreated to save his Army,
Out-distanced "Corn" 'cross Carolina,
And even crossed Virginia's line.

And as he raced for Virginia,
In his desperate plight,
Greene chose hills near Guilford Courthouse,
For a later fighting sight.

He won the race for Virginia,
Then rested and drilled his men;
"Corn" stopped and pillaged 'til Spring in North Carolina
And fumed for a knock-out win.

Mid-March, seventeen eighty-one,
To do or die all valor 'rouse,
Greene moved back South to crack "Old Corn,"
To the hills near Guilford Courthouse.

Greene formed his men in three straight lines,
A quarter mile apart
(While baiting "Corn" to come and fight),
Entrenched for the Battle's start.

"Corn" marched down the New Garden Road,
Red Coats in step to the drum;
The sentries' shots began to pop,
And the battle began to hum.

Their Guards, with crushing drive and power,
Blasted our rights and centers,
A half mile east toward the Courthouse,
As furiously all men struggled.

Our first two lines, first fired, with effect, then gave,
Before "Corn's" heavy power,
Recruits against the Royal Vets—
Will the Battle last an hour?

Greene's third line crouched just over a hill;
Can our Veterans stop their power?
They march on with that British will,
To make it their finest hour.

Up from the brush, our third line 'rose,
And aimed a withering fire
That piled up "Red Coats" down the hill,
And forced the live ones back, as,

Greene's cavalry under William Washington,
With lust for blood and gore,
Then swooped through King George's men
And shrieked a Hellish roar.

Young "Pete," a horseman, galloped hard,
And slashed, with his broad sword waving.
Men fell to the left and right of him;
His kill had soon reached seven.

Still closing in, "Pete" killed three more,
'Til engulfed—both horse and rider fell,
But he madly struggled up again,
And sought to fight off Hell.

A lance pinned "Pete's" leg fast to his horse;
Good luck had now had its fill.
He was a sitting duck for the British Guard,
Who readied his sword for the kill.

"Pete" stood lance-pinned, to his dead steed,
As his broad sword reflected the sun,
That o'ersized gift from Valley Forge,
Of General Washington.

"Pete" used swift art, at the thrust 'round his back;
The scene became gory with red.
"Pete" quick backstroked with his long broad sword,
And cut off his enemy's head.

And while our cavalry riding hard,
Knocked them yet down the slope,
"Old Corn" was thrown off his horse,
Their Lion—the British Hope.

But up from shame "Corn" struggled hard,
To stop this quick retreat,
At frantic "Red Coats" scampered past,
Convinced of his sure defeat.

"For King George, our heaviest guns,"
Fast bellowed, Cornwallis.
"Fire straight into all moving men
(Too bad if we kill our own)."

His cannon killed both friend and foe,
But his backward movement stopped;
Greene's third line slipped from the cannonade,
Back East by Guilford Courthouse.

And Greene, not risking his army more,
Directed a general retreat,
Repaired intact to the Iron Works,
Left Cornwallis in crippling defeat.

"Corn" hobbled for the King, as he took the field—
His dead fairly covered the ground;
'Twas here he caught a killing blow,
Foretelling "Quits" at Yorktown.

Epilogue

And Pete Francisco was nursed back and fought on,
'Til our Nation won independence,
Then lived near Richmond, Virginia, to a ripe old age,
And has left hundreds of living descendants.

The Valley Dale Wreck*

They phoned him on his fast run
Near Center, South Carolina,
Saying, "Duff, you're sixty minutes late.
This is not an ancient 'Steam Job' like Old 97,
But Modern Diesel 68."

So he hollered 'cross the cab
To his Fireman, Fillups,
"From now, we're makin' up that hour,
And when we reach the grade the other side of Tri-Point,
I'll be needing all your Diesel Power."

There's a mighty steep grade
From Tri-Point to Grimtown,
Past Grimtown, crossings as well;
'Twas on the latter segment, that he had his adventure,
And this is his story to tell:

He blew his whistle down the grade,
Running at ninety miles an hour,
And you could hear that long train's bell.
He hit the Agger's auto at the Valley Dale Crossing,
And crushed 'em to a quick farewell.

Now, John Q. Public, you must take warning
From this event and learn—
Never guess your auto-mobile
Upon a Diesel Grade Crossing,
Or you may leave home and never return.

---

*Sing to the tune of "The Wreck of Old 97."

The Criminal Term (Long Ago)

Many cases had already been tried.
The Solicitor next called the
Homicide Case of John La Mar:
Murder in the First Degree, of Mizzes
J. P. McGrann, to wit,
The killing of this brave little
Mother, while tending her family's filling
Station on the Tri-Point Highway;
When held up by the defendant,
She grabbed her pistol and shot
Back at him, but fell soon and died,
Shot through the body many times.
The jury was finally selected.
A two-day trial ensued.
A man identified La Mar.
La Mar gambled an alibi:
That he was elsewhere; took the stand,
Cap in hand, and lied. But soon the Solicitor
Broke the defendant's alibi;
And he admitted that, with gun
In pocket and that same old cap
Upon his head, he walked up
About the time the shots began.
His Honor charged the Jury
For two full hours; it was out for three,
Came back, found John guilty
Of Murder in the First Degree—
And soon thereafter, with great finality,
His Honor said, "Stand up, La Mar!
La Mar, have you aught to say as
To why sentence should not be passed
On you as provided by law?"
"Mercy, please, Mister Judge," begged
La Mar, with sobs. "But such here is

Beyond my powers," said the Judge.
"It is certainly not the Judge,
Solicitor, or Jury, but
The Law which now sentences you—
You brought yourself to the hot spot;
You should have had mercy on that
Brave little Lady defending
Her filling station and children,
And not riddled her with bullets,
Dispirited her young husband,
And orphaned her three little babes.
This is the sentence of the Court:
You, John La Mar, shall be immediately conveyed,
By the Sheriff of Cranford County, to Raleigh, North Carolina,
And there turned over to the Warden of our
State Penitentiary, who shall well and truly keep you,
Until the time for the execution of this sentence—
Two months and three days hence, to wit,
On the ———day of———, ———, said Warden,
Of our State Penitentiary,
After placing you in a chair, as provided by law,
Shall cause to course through your body,
With great rapidity,
A current of high-powered electricity,
Which shall be continued until
You shall be pronounced dead, dead, dead,
And may God have mercy on your soul.
Except for his own weeping wails,
A total stillness filled the room,
As John La Mar was led toward doom.

At Another Criminal Term (In the Distant Past)

Next was tried the case of Willie Lure,
Well known locally, to be sure,
For the fortieth time—Charge: Public Drunkenness.
He pleaded Not Guilty: Officer Bell
Was sworn and took the stand;
"He was drunk at Elm and Edwards."
Willie then went on and swore
He had only drunk one bottle of beer,
And said he staggered as he walked when sober.
The jury quickly found him guilty—
Willie, in the manner of a trained lawyer,
Jumped up from his seat, exclaiming,
"Your Honor, I hope you will not hold
It against me because I did
Not enter a Plea in this case!"
The Judge said, "I hold that a Judge
Is justified in extending
Leniency to a guilty man
Who pleads Guilty, and in *burning
Up* one who is clearly guilty
Beyond all doubt, yet appeals from City Court and takes up the
Court's time with a contested trial,
As he usurps the stand to lie."
"Your Honor, give me one more chance,
And you will never see me in
Court again." Said the Judge, "My heart
Is with you, but my decision,
Is against you."
(Laughter in the room.)
"You have loved the

Bars, lo, these many years, as you
Have drunk strong drink and thereafter collapsed
In public; for the next six
Months your ideal shall be a fact!

You, Lure, are to be surrounded
By different *bars* at night, and through the day,
Your range embracing wider scope,
You shall wear stripes, break rocks, build roads!
For your own good, let it inure—
Rebuild yourself by the Working Cure."
(Light smiles emanated from the crowd.)

At Still Another Criminal Term (Many Years Ago)

"Call another case, Mr. Solicitor."
"Yes, Your Honor, State against Lucy Street."
She was a plump prostitute
Caught in the "Act" in a raid on
The well-known Gilfine Hotel.
She was a three-time offender, once good looking,
With hair dirty-colored and uncombed. Plea: Guilty.
She stood and commenced pacing
Sideways and back before the Bench.
With brazen tones, she bluntly said,
"Please, Judge, I had to live somehow."
"But you didn't have to live that way."
(People snickered in the Courtroom.)
"Mercy, Judge, mercy, let me go—
I'll sure be good, and always behave.
I won't harm no one, nowhere, Judge.
And I'll go to Church sometimes too."
"Woman, the Good People of Cranford
County are hungry for your absence."

"Let me go! I won't never do
It again, SIR." More laughter
Filled the Courtroom. Quoth His Honor,
"But I must give Relief to
THE GOOD PEOPLE OF CRANFORD COUNTY—
Mister Clerk, my sentence is
One year at Cranford County Home—
To work as provided by Law—
Prison Sentence suspended, if
She shall go away from North Carolina
By nine A.M. tomorrow morn and get lawful work,
And stay away for fifteen years—
Capias to issue if she returns
During said next fifteen years."

At the Criminal Term—The Last Case (An Ancient Term)

Next was the case of Warley Wells—
The Charge: "Fraudulent Disposal
Of Mortgaged Personal Property,
To wit, a certain mule."
The defendant was brought down from
The Cranford Jail by a sheriff.
Plea: Not Guilty. A jury was selected.
Jed Bolo, representing the
Private prosecution, showed,
By witnesses for the State,
That the defendant mortgaged
Said mule to his client, Hardutt, who loaned money,
For Two Hundred Dollars—and then two months later,
Mortgaged to John Hall for the sum of One Hundred Dollars;
There was a default in payment;
Hardutt started to foreclose,
But found Hall's mortgage ahead of him and quit.

Cross-examination showed Jed Bolo's client
Never recorded his first mortgage,
But the second, with a very light line through the warranties,
Was recorded by Hall.
Then the State rested.

Glade Hedrickson, for the defendant,
Then moved for Judgment as of Non-Suit, saying,
"They've showed no criminal or wicked intent,
And proved no hurt to Hardutt, who loans money,
By 'Young' Wells, whom they've thrown in jail.
The warranties were stricken in Hall's mortgage,
They nefariously seek to turn
Your Honor's Great Criminal Superior Court
Into a blood-sucking collection agency—
A diabolical procedure and an unethical
Use of the Criminal Courts.
They choose dangerous waters, for even the
Boldest 'Loan Sharks' dare usually flap no deeper,
Than the shallow, filthy ponds
Of certain shady Criminal J. P. Courts."
"Have you made out a case against him?"
Asked the Judge. "Was there any
Criminal intent? The defendant
Could give many mortgages,
If without fraud. Why didn't the State's witness
Think to record his first mortgage?
The second mortgage has the warranties stricken;
The mule may be worth more than both mortgages.
No one has shown that he is ill, or that he can't bray!
Is there sufficient proof the clever State's witness has been
Taken on a financial 'Snipe Hunt'?
I find no statutory fault in this young man."
Said Mr. Bolo, "If Your Honor
Now doubts his guilt, then just deny
The Motion made by Mr. Hedrickson, so
I can make him take the witness

Stand and cross-examine him, and I'll show his clever fraud.
And then you will have no further
Cause to doubt his being guilty.
There are cases holding contra;
There are many fine points that are difficult to know."
"Yes," said the Judge. "You are quite right;
There are many many things in
This old world, that I don't know,
But I tell you, LAW 'AIN'T ONE OF 'EM' "
(Great laughter from the entire Courtroom).
Said Bolo, while still persisting,
"Will Your Honor not temporarily
Bypass the non-suit motion,
So he will have to take the witness stand?"
"Do you infer there's a Pilate
On this good Cranford Bench?" frowned
The Judge. "Shall I take away his constitutional rights?
I find no fault in him.
I wash my hands of all his blood.
But that's not all; Pilate did that much. He shall go free."
And facing the defendant, said,
"Go breathe the free air of Cranford,
Deeply, like Greene breathed, when
He fought Cornwallis at Guilford Courthouse,
Dealt him the crippling blow,
In mid-March seventeen eighty-one,
Proximately causing his collapse
At Yorktown, seven months, four days later."
At this juncture, the defendant,
Though stunned by the sudden turn of events,
Arose, bowed to his Honor, shook hands with his lawyer,
Then quickly left the Courtroom.
Outside, as he passed into the fresh air,
He breathed chesty as a robin.
The Judge, facing the Solicitor, asked,
"Are there any more cases for the term, Mr. Solicitor?"
"No, Your Honor." "You may adjourn Court Sine Die, Sheriff."

And the sheriff, again raising his gray
Handlebar mustache and shaking his
Gorgeous head of hair, intoned through two missing front teeth,
"Everybody stand! O Yez, O Yez,
Dis honorable Court now adjourns sine die;
God save de State and dis honorable Court."
As people began leaving Court,
The Judge (with a twinkle in his eye) scolded the Sheriff,
By whispering in a low voice
Over the Bench, "Sheriff, you are
The only man in this County
Who can publicly call me
Dishonorable, but you call me
Just that, twice in the morning when you open Court
And twice in the afternoon when you close,
And always get away with it."
Smiled the Sheriff, through his gray handlebars,
"Now, Judge, you know I never wrote
Them speeches, yet two times today
You ordered me to recite 'em—
I launched you safely this morning.
I landed you this afternoon.
All day you soared like an EAGLE."
And there with this strike back, ended the Judge's attack.

Down the steps to the Judge's Chamber
Cane in hand, heading home with a glow.
Remember, GOOD PEOPLE OF CRANFORD,
COURT WEEK, in the long, long ago.

Index of Names and Titles

Appomattox, 11
At Another Criminal Term (In the Distant Past), 90-91
At Still Another Criminal Term (Many Years Ago), 91-92
At the Criminal Term—The Last Case (An Ancient Term), 92-95

Back in the Good Old Days, 63
Bob Fitzsimmons, 47-50
Boston Common, 27
Burns, Robert, 14

Candidate for the Senate, The, 43
College Student's Song about Greensboro Colleges, A, 15
Constitution, The, 51-56
Criminal Term (Long Ago), The, 88-89
Crude, Occo, 65-67

Descent to the Moon, The, 42

Early Spring, 71
Easter, 44
Eastern Regional Tournament, The, 38
Fitzsimmons, Bob, 47-50
Francisco, Peter, 18, 19, 82-86

Glenn, John, 75-76
Grant, Ulysses S., 11
Great World Christmas Tree, A, 72
Greene, Nathanael, 82-85
Greensboro, 18-19
Guilford Courthouse, Battle of, 82-86

Halloween, on an Old Streetcar, 64
High Point—Greensboro Furniture Dealers' Song, 22-23
Higher Law, 35

Introduction, 9

Judge Lon McGraw, 65-67

Lee, Robert E., 11, 77
Lincoln, Abraham, 11

March at Jefferson Square, 17
Miller, Mary Lou, 23-24
Mockingbird, The, 16

Moon Landing, The, 41
Mortal You, 34
Mount Airy Train, The, 39

Navy's Norfolk, Virginia, B.O.Q., S.P. 17, 21
1952 Presidential Race and Former Races, The, 79-82
Number Thirty-six, 12

On the Law, the Universal Law, 28
On the Way to the Moon, 40
Old Pomona Streetcar Line at Greensboro, 57-62
Our United Nations, 46

Peter Francisco and Guilford Courthouse, 82-86
Preddy, George E., Jr., 18-19

Reading Prodigy, The, 23-24
Robert Burns, 14

Said, 25
Scott, W. Kerr, 43
Sedgefield Fox Hunt, 13
Snow Blizzard, 68-69
Spaceman John Glenn's Ride, 75-76
Spread of Law, The, 29-30
Spring from the Southeastern Building, 37

Tennessee Volunteers of 1951, 26
That Day, 73-75
Those Interplanetary Men, 41
Train Trip, The, 31-33
Two-Way Elm, 70-71

Unite, 45
United Nations, 46

Valley Dale Wreck, The, 87
Virginia, 78-79

Washington, 20-21
Washington, George, 20-21, 53, 77, 81, 84
Washington and Lee, 77
Westward Friendly, Ho!, 36-37